Share It!

Instagram Projects for the Real World

Rebecca Felix

Checkerboard Library

An Imprint of Abdo Publishing
abdopublishing.com

abdopublishing.com

Published by Abdo Publishing, a division of ABDO, PO Box 398166, Minneapolis, Minnesota 55439. Copyright © 2017 by Abdo Consulting Group, Inc. International copyrights reserved in all countries. No part of this book may be reproduced in any form without written permission from the publisher. Checkerboard Library™ is a trademark and logo of Abdo Publishing.

Printed in the United States of America, North Mankato, Minnesota

062016
092016

THIS BOOK CONTAINS
RECYCLED MATERIALS

Content Developer: Nancy Tuminelly
Design and Production: Mighty Media, Inc.
Series Editor: Liz Salzmann
Photo Credits: AP Images; Mighty Media, Inc.; Shutterstock; Wikimedia Commons

The following manufacturers/names appearing in this book are trademarks: 3M™, Artist's Loft™, Elmer's®, Sharpie®

Publishers Cataloging-in-Publication Data
Names: Felix, Rebecca, author.
Title: Share it! : Instagram projects for the real world / by Rebecca Felix.
Description: Minneapolis, MN : Abdo Publishing, [2017] | Series: Cool social
    media | Includes bibliographical references and index.
Identifiers: LCCN 2016936500 | ISBN 9781680783599 (lib. bdg.) |
    ISBN 9781680790276 (ebook)
Subjects: LCSH: Instagram (Firm)--Juvenile literature. | Online social networks--
    Juvenile literature. | Photography--Digital techniques--Juvenile literature. |
    Image processing--Digital techniques--Juvenile literature. | Internet industry--
    United States--Juvenile literature. | Internet security measures--Juvenile
    literature.
Classification: DDC 775--dc23
LC record available at /http://lccn.loc.gov/2016936500

Contents

What Is
Instagram?

You're playing fetch with your dog in the park. She runs toward you with the tennis ball in her mouth. It looks as though she's smiling! You decide you must take a picture. You reach for your smartphone and shoot the scene. You add a **filter** that makes the ball's bright yellow really pop. Then you ask your dad to post the photo to Instagram. Your family's followers like and comment on it. Then their followers see your puppy picture too. This is Instagram at work!

Instagram is a photo- and video-sharing website and app. Users post photos they've taken. But first, many alter their photos using Instagram's **unique** editing tools.

Instagrammers post pictures to their accounts. Any users who follow the posters see these photos. Interaction between users is an important part of the Instagram community. Users can tag one another to communicate. They can also comment on photos and add hashtags. If a user likes or comments on another user's photos, all of his or her followers will also see the photos. In this way, Instagram photos can go **viral**!

Instagram
Site Bytes

Purpose: sharing photos and videos

Type of Service: website and app
URL: www.instagram.com
App name: Instagram

Date of Founding: October 6, 2010

Founders: Kevin Systrom, Mike Krieger

Compatible Devices:

Tablet   Smartphone   Laptop

Tech Terms:

Hashtags

Hashtags are added to photo and video **captions** and comments. A hashtag is a hash symbol (#) followed by a word or phrase. The hashtag becomes a link that groups photos together. Clicking on a hashtag takes the user to all posts using that hashtag.

Filters

Instagrammers use **filters** to alter the color of their images. Instagram also has tools that change an image's focus, brightness, tilt, contrast, and more.

Founding **Instagram**

Kevin Systrom and Mike Krieger met at Stanford University in California. After college, Systrom got an idea for a new app. He asked Krieger to work on it with him.

The app Krieger and Systrom created was called Burbn. It allowed users to play games, share photos, and more. Sharing photos was the feature used most often. So, Krieger and Systrom changed the app to focus on shooting, editing, and sharing photos on **mobile** phones. They renamed the app Instagram. It launched in October 2010. By 2015, Instagram had more than 400 million users!

Mike Krieger

Kevin Systrom

Account Info:

- Users must be at least 13 to create an account.
- Once a user creates an account, he or she chooses a username and **uploads** a profile photo.
- Users find other Instagrammers to follow, searching for them by name, username, or topic.
- Users can set their profiles to public or private.
- Anyone can view public accounts.
- Only users with accounts can like or comment on images.
- If a user likes or comments on a public account, all of his or her followers will then see the image that user liked or commented on.
- Only users accepted as followers can see, like, and comment on a private user's photos.

Supplies

Here are some of the materials, tools, and devices you'll need to do the projects in this book.

colored cellophane

photo frame

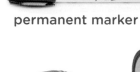

permanent marker

wet-erase markers

string

duct tape

world map

printer (loaded with paper and ink)

magnetic tape

sticky notes

scissors

tablet

smartphone

Staying Safe

The Internet is a great resource for information. And using it can be a lot of fun! But staying safe **online** is most important. Follow these tips to use social media safely.

* Never try to sign up for a social media account if you are underage. Instagram users must be at least 13 years old.

* Don't share personal information online, especially information people can use to find you in real life. This includes your telephone number and home address.

* Be kind online! Remember that real people post content on the Internet. Do not post rude, hurtful, or mean comments. Report any instances of **cyberbullying** you see to a trusted adult.

* In addition to cyberbullying, report any **inappropriate** content to a trusted adult.

Safety Symbols

Some projects in this book require searching on the Internet. Others require the use of sharp tools. That means these projects need some adult help. Determine if you'll need help on a project by looking for these safety symbols.

Internet Use
This project requires searching on the Internet.

Sharp!
This project requires use of sharp tools.

Frame Filters

Cut colored filters to fit a photo frame and instantly alter a photo!

What you need

- » photo frame
- » colored cellophane
- » permanent markers
- » scissors
- » photo that fits in the frame

1. Disassemble the frame. Carefully trace the glass on several sheets of cellophane.

2. Cut out the cellophane. Reassemble the frame. Place a cellophane cutout between the glass and photo. You've made a printed photo inspired by Instagram! The cellophane **mimics** the effects of an Instagram **filter**.

3. Experiment by using different colors of cellophane. Or layer two colors over your image at once. Try creating your own effects. Draw designs on a light-colored or clear piece of cellophane with permanent markers.

4. Store the extra cellophane cutouts between the photo and frame back. Change the filter whenever you like!

#funfact

Instagram has 27 filters. Each alters the appearance of an image in a different way.

Magnetic Photo Frames

Create Instagram-inspired frames to hang on the fridge!

#BESTFRIENDS

#CUTEPUPPY

What you need

- » computer
- » printer
- » photos to print
- » scissors
- » craft foam
- » pencil
- » ruler
- » craft knife
- » scrap cardboard
- » permanent markers in several colors
- » magnetic tape

1. Print a photo from your computer. It can be your own photo or one you find **online** with adult help.

2. Trim the photo into a square. The frame will cover part of the edges, so leave a little extra around the outside.

3. Trace the photo on craft foam. Set the photo aside. Draw a smaller square within the square you just traced. The smaller square should be ½ inch (1.3 cm) in from each edge of the larger square.

4. Cut the large squares out of the foam. Then place the foam square on top of the cardboard. Have an adult help cut out the smaller square with the craft knife.

5. Pick a hashtag for the photo. Write it on your frame.

6. Cut a strip of magnetic tape. Stick it to the back of the frame.

7. Use the frame to hang your photo on the refrigerator!

Insta-Cards

Craft cool collections of images to make
Instagram-inspired greeting cards!

#CUPCAKE

#PARTY

#SISTERS

#FUN

#HAPPYBIRTHDAY

#PARTY

Happy Birthday!

What you need

- » computer
- » word-processing program
- » printer
- » scissors
- » card stock
- » glue stick
- » marker

1. Use a computer to find six images for the card. They can be your own photos or ones you find **online** with adult help.

2. Drag the images onto a word-processing page. Use the program's editing tools to make each photo 2½ inches (6.3 cm) square.

3. Print the photos. Cut them out.

4. Fold a piece of card stock in half to create a card. Arrange the photos in a **grid** on the front of the card. Space them evenly.

5. Glue the photos in place.

6. Fill out and decorate the card. Write a hashtag under each image, such as #happybirthday, #birthdaywishes, and more.

TIP: If you plan to sell your cards, use only your own photos. Make sure any people in the photos have agreed to be on your cards.

Instagram Image Bingo

**Make bingo cards of Instagram image topics.
Then go on an online scavenger hunt!**

1. Write "BINGO" at the top of a piece of paper. Use the pencil and ruler to draw a large square under the word. Draw lines to make a **grid** that is five squares wide and five squares high.

2. Use the ruler to trace over the grid lines in marker.

3. Write "FREE" in the grid's center square.

4. Choose a topic from the list below. Write the Instagram sites for the topic on the back of the grid.

Space
NASA: @nasa, instagram.com/nasa/
International Space Station: @iss, instagram.com/iss/
Kennedy Space Center: @kennedyspacecenter, instagram.com/kennedyspacecenter/

Animals
Animal Planet: @animalplanet, instagram.com/animalplanet/
World Wildlife Federation: @wwf, instagram.com/wwf/
Nature on PBS: @pbsnature, instagram.com/pbsnature/

Movies and Television
Disney: @disney, instagram.com/disney/
Pixar: @pixar, instagram.com/pixar/
Nickelodeon: @nickelodeontv, instagram.com/nickelodeontv/

(continued on the next page)

5. Then visit the Instagram sites for the topic you chose. What images related to the topic do you see on these sites? Make a list of 24 items shown in the images.

6. Fill in the **grid** with the 24 items from your list. Write one item in each square. Place the bingo card in the page protector.

7. Make more bingo cards. Write the items on your list in different squares on each card.

8. To play the game, give each player a bingo card and a wet-erase marker. Each player will also need a computer, tablet, or smartphone.

9. Have the players search the Instagram sites to find the items on the card. They should cross out the items as they find them. The first one to find five in a row wins!

10. Use a damp tissue or cloth to clean the marks from the page protector. Then, play again! Try making bingo cards on different topics. See who can search Instagram the fastest.

9

10

Filter Flip-Book

Fashion a flip-book that demonstrates how Instagram's editing tools alter images.

What you need

» computer
» printer
» scissors
» marker
» sandpaper
» colored cellophane
» clear tape
» wax paper
» stapler
» duct tape

Instagram allows users to edit their images in several ways. These include **filters**, which can alter the color, tint, and overall look of an image. Other editing tools can alter brightness, warmth, contrast, and shadows. Users can also fade an image, make it look old, give its edges a burned look, and much more. These tools can transform photos into interesting artworks. But they also show viewers an altered reality. See how much these effects can change an image by making a flip-book that **mimics** Instagram's editing tools.

1. Choose an image to print. It can be your own photo or one you find **online** with adult help. Print four copies of the photo.

2. Cut out each photo.

3. Number the backs of the photos 1 through 4. Set photo 1 aside.

4. Lightly sand images 2, 3, and 4. Then set photo 2 aside.

(continued on the next page)

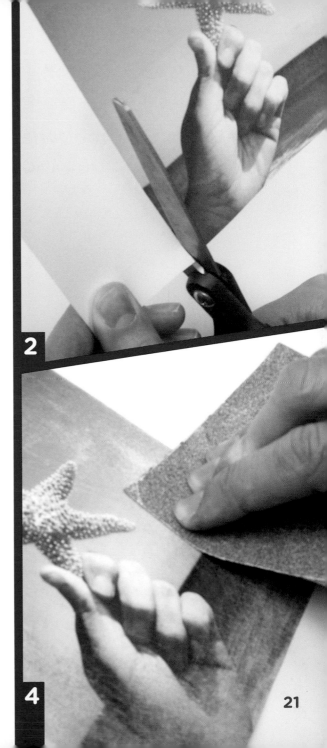

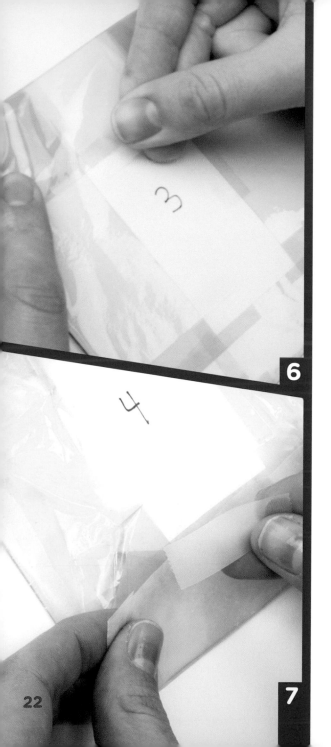

5. Cut two pieces of cellophane a little larger than the photos. Both should be the same color.

6. Wrap a piece of cellophane around photo 3. Tape the edges to the back of the photo. Cover photo 4 with the other piece of cellophane the same way. Set photo 3 aside.

7. Cut a piece of wax paper a little larger than the photos. Wrap it around photo 4 over the cellophane. Tape the edges to the back of the photo.

8. **Stack** all photos in numerical order, with photo 1 on top.

9. Staple the photos together along the left edge. Wrap a piece of duct tape around the edge over the staples.

10. Flip through the book. How different is photo 4 from photo 1? Do you think Instagram's editing tools affect images more or less than the physical **filters** and effects you created?

8

9

Viral Reveal

Create an interactive poster that mimics how photos go viral on Instagram!

What you need
» large image from a magazine or old calendar
» poster board
» glue stick
» markers
» ruler
» sticky notes, small
» sticky notes, large
» string
» scissors
» hole punch

When people post photos on Instagram, their followers can see them. If a follower likes or comments on an image, it becomes visible to his or her followers too. The more people interact with an image, the more visible it becomes to others.

1. Choose a picture for your poster. The picture should be large. It could be a full-page photo from a magazine. Or it could be a large photo from an old calendar.

2. Glue the image to the top half of the poster board.

3. Beneath the image, write, "If you like this photo, move a ♥ into the likes box. If you want to comment, write one on a blue sticky note and move it into the comments box."

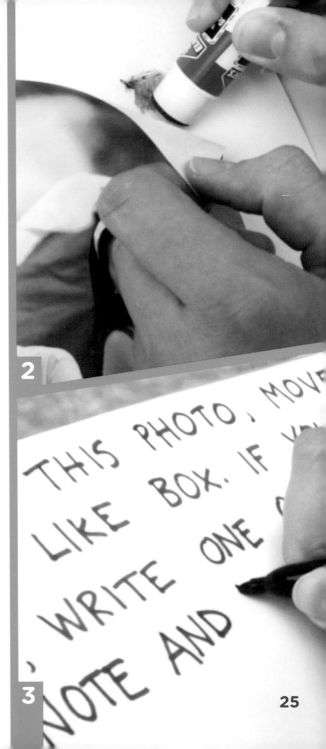

(continued on the next page)

4. Use a ruler and a marker to draw a large box under the text. Draw a vertical line down the middle of the box. Write "likes" at the top of the left side. Write "comments" at the top of the right side.

5. Draw a red heart on each small sticky note. This is the symbol for "like" on Instagram. Draw a blue hashtag and line on each large sticky note. Instagrammers often comment on images using hashtags.

6. Cover most of the photo with small and large sticky notes. Choose a small but interesting part of the photo to leave uncovered. This will give the first person to see the photo something to like or comment on.

#funfact
More than half of all Instagram posts have at least one hashtag.

7. Cut a long piece of string. Tie one end to a marker.

8. Punch a hole at the bottom of the poster. Tie the other end of the string to the hole. Viewers will use the marker to write hashtag comments on the large sticky notes.

9. Ask for **permission** to hang the poster at home or school. As people like and comment on the image, more of it will be uncovered. How fast was the entire image revealed? The more people interacted with the image, the more visible it became, just like on Instagram!

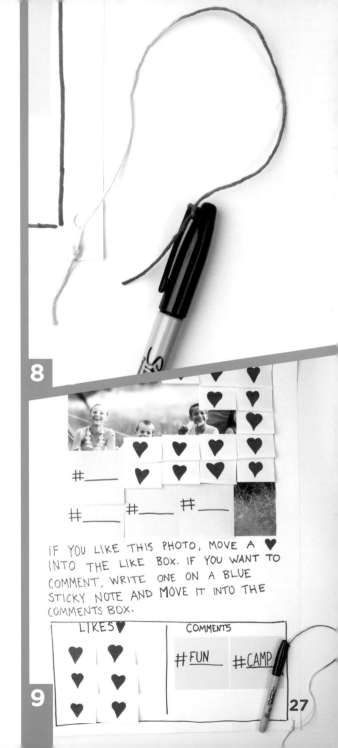

8

9

IF YOU LIKE THIS PHOTO, MOVE A ♥ INTO THE LIKE BOX. IF YOU WANT TO COMMENT, WRITE ONE ON A BLUE STICKY NOTE AND MOVE IT INTO THE COMMENTS BOX.

LIKES ♥	COMMENTS	
♥ ♥	#FUN	#CAMP
♥ ♥		
♥ ♥		

Geography Gallery

Create a map showing cool places around the world!

What you need

- » world map
- » computer
- » printer
- » large piece of cardboard
- » newspaper
- » acrylic paint
- » foam brush
- » craft glue
- » photos of places you have been or would like to visit
- » scissors
- » colored card stock
- » hole punch
- » string
- » thumbtacks

1. Get a world map. It could already be printed. Or have an adult help you find one **online** and print it out.

2. Cut the cardboard so it is a little bigger than the map. Cover your work surface with newspaper. Paint the cardboard. Let the paint dry.

3. Glue the map to the cardboard.

4. Print photos from your computer. They can be your own photos or ones you find online with adult help. Look for pictures of buildings, monuments, parks, cities, and countries.

#funfact

Until 2015, all Instagram images were square. In August of that year, the company began allowing rectangular photos and videos.

(continued on the next page)

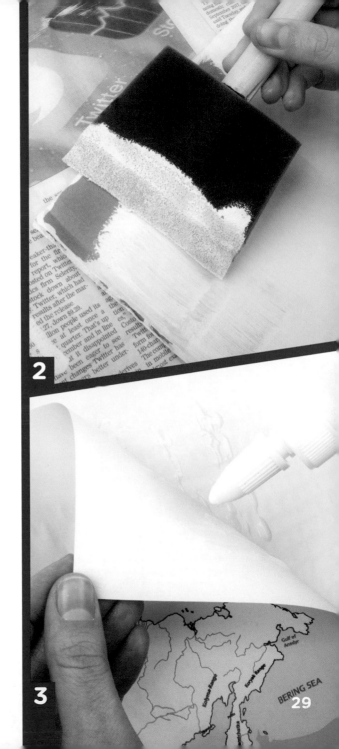

2

3

29

5. Trim the photos into squares. Glue them onto the colored card stock. Cut out the photos, leaving a colored border around their edges.

6. Punch a hole in the top of a photo. Cut a short piece of string and thread it through the hole. Tie the string in a knot to make a loop. Repeat for all photos.

7. Stick a tack into each of your chosen locations on the map. Hang each image from the tack marking its location.

8. Hang your geographic gallery in your room. Add photos as you visit new places or as you discover new spots you want to see!

Glossary

caption – a written explanation of an image, such as a photo.

cyberbully – to tease, hurt, or threaten someone online.

filter – a tool that can change the appearance of a photo.

grid – a pattern with rows of squares, such as a checkerboard.

inappropriate – not suitable, fitting, or proper.

mimic – to imitate or copy.

mobile – capable of moving or being moved.

online – connected to the Internet.

permission – when a person in charge says it's okay to do something.

stack – to put things on top of each other.

unique – not the same as anything else.

upload – to transfer data from a computer to a larger network.

viral – quickly or widely spread, usually by electronic communication.

Websites

To learn more about Cool Social Media, visit **booklinks.abdopublishing.com**. These links are routinely monitored and updated to provide the most current information available.

Index